Arduino

Learn how to Create Interactive Electronic Objects, Setting up your Board, Discover how Coding Works, Create your Circuit plus all the essentials of Arduino Programming (For Beginners)

Julian James McKinnon

Table of Contents

Introduction

Congratulations on purchasing **Arduino Programming for Beginners**, and thank you for doing so.

The following chapters will discuss all of the different parts that we need to know when it is time to work with the Arduino microcontroller.

There are a lot of tools that we are able to focus on when it is time to handle our work in technology and learning how to program, but none are going to provide us with the same benefits and more that we can find when working with the Arduino system.

This guidebook is going to dive into this controller and take a look at some of the ways that we are able to utilize it for our needs.

This guidebook is going to take a look at some of the basics that we are able to handle when it comes to the Arduino controller.

We will look a bit more at some of the histories of working with Arduino, what this controller is, who will use this program and some of the advantages of choosing this controller overall.

Then we can move on to some of the key terms that we need to focus on, such as the anatomy of our board, to ensure that we can actually use this the right way.

Once all of that is done, it is time for us to go through and look at how to set up our Arduino board and make it work for our own needs.

We will spend some time learning more about how to pick out a board, how to run Arduino, how to do some of the codings, and so much more.

And that leads us right into some of the basics of coding in Arduino, such as the syntax, the structure, and the different data types before exploring the basics of turning this controller into the machine that we want to use.

We will also bring up a bit about the C language in this guidebook, and how we are able to utilize this to help us get ahead.

There are a lot of options that we can explore when it comes to coding with this board, but the C language is going to be one of the best options for its ease of use and the fact that it is similar to the Arduino language that we will discuss as well.

From there, we are going to spend some time looking at a few of the other things that we can do with this language and this controller.

We will look at how to do the logic statements, how to handle our own operators, how to work with some of the work that we need to handle when doing computer interfacing, the idea of the different API functions, and how to work with the streaming class on this controller.

We can then end this guidebook with a discussion of how to create our user-defined functions so that we can really get the most out of our new coding tool.

There are a lot of different parts that we are able to work with when it comes to the Arduino controller and all of the neat things that it is able to help us accomplish.

When we are ready to learn more about how the Arduino board and controller can work and what all we are able to do with it, make sure to check out this guidebook to help us get started.

There are plenty of books on this subject on the market, thanks again for choosing this one!

Every effort was made to ensure it is full of as much useful information as possible; please enjoy it!

Chapter 1: The Basics to Know About Arduino

We are currently in a huge age of technology right now, and there is always a lot more and increasing amounts of technological literacy that even the average person is expected to have, much more than what was required in the past.

More and more people are learning the terms and how to use the variety of software and hardware that is available to them out there, and there is even more interest overtime for them to work on some of these things, whether they want to do it more as a professional or as a hobby.

During these changes, it is common for a lot of new programmers to be attracted to what we can find with the Arduino system.

Maybe you have seen a few of the different projects that this system is able to do for us, or you might have just had a chance to hear about it and how some of the flexibility and ease of use can make life a little bit easier overall.

No matter the case for you, you will find that there are a lot of benefits that come with using the Arduino system for your own needs as well.

Keeping some of these ideas in mind, we need to spend some time going into more details about what the Arduino system is all about, how we can work with some of the technology, and how we are able to make all of this provide us with the benefits we want in the process.

First, though, we need to spend our time looking at a bit of the history of this technology.

The Arduino History

First, we need to look more at some of the histories that are going to come with the Arduino device.

The technology that showed up with this started as just a basic idea back in 2003. Hernando Barragan wanted to come up with a system that could simplify the way that the BASIC stamp microcontroller was going to work, while still making sure that there was a reduction in some of the costs that come with it.

This would make it easier for some of the engineer students to purchase and work with this technology, without all the huge costs.

To start with on this one, the Arduino microcontroller is going to be a smaller board on a computer that we are able to program and work with in order to perform some of the different functions that we need at the time.

In 2003, most of these controllers cost at least $100, and often they would be more if you would like to have some special features to handle it.

But this is not true when we work with the Arduino system.

These are going to reduce a lot of the costs that you are able to see with these controllers without breaking the bank.

This technology was developed and changed throughout time, and by 2013, there were about 700,000 microcontroller boards that were sold from the Adafruit Industries alone, a New York City supplier of these boards.

While there were some issues that come with the trademarking of the Arduino, which ended up with a split inside of the company for a few years, Arduino is now going to be one single company that has devoted itself to the development of software and hardware that is usable by the average person, while still having enough flexibility in it to interest professional engineers.

What is Arduino?

This is going to bring us to the question of what the Arduino board is all about.

The history of Arduino sounds a bit confusing right now, but the good thing to consider is that it is not going to be all as complicated as it seems right now.

We are able to go through at this point and learn a bit more about the whole system in place, what it is able to do for us, and more as we go through this whole guidebook.

The first part of this that we are going to explore is how the Arduino board is going to work.

You first need to go out and purchase the hardware, choosing the option that will fit with what your goals are on this project.

And then, with the help of another computer that has one of the other major operating systems on it, whether we are talking about Mac, Linux, or Windows, you are going to spend some time writing out the right codes with instructions to the board, uploading all of the steps and instructions that you want the board to follow through the codes that you are writing along the way.

The code that you write in this process will be stored in the microcontroller, and it is going to function based on these instructions any time that you call them up.

The neat thing with this kind of board is that you are able to write out any of the instructions that you would like, and they are going to work.

You could do it to have a beep sound off when you start up the controller or even have it work when it senses light.

This is simply a way to practice some of the basics of coding along the way, and there are so many options that you are really able to explore to make this happens.

Who Will Work with Arduino?

You may even be surprised by some of the different people who will work with the Arduino board and can find it useful for their needs.

There are a lot of people who will bring out this controller to work on their projects, whether these are for work or as a hobby.

And there are even some professionals who want to work with this as well. Because all of the programming on this one is simple and straightforward to work with for a beginner, and rich enough so that the beginner is able to learn some skills and grow into more complicated things, later on, this board, in particular, has grown in popularity over time.

It will not take long using this system before you notice that there are a lot of people who like to work with it.

Teachers and students like to work with this one, and indeed it is going to be one of the main consumer bases of this kind of product.

They were designed to be a low-cost method that is going to help us t build up some of our own scientific instruments so that teachers and students can do demonstrations and practices in chemistry and physics and so many other parts as well.

In addition, we will find that there are other individuals who will utilize this for their needs as well.

Designers and architects can use this in order to help them build p the interactive prototypes and models that they want over time, allowing them to view what is going to happen as they add and take away things.

Musicians and artists are even able to work with these to do some experiments with new techniques and instruments based on what they would like to accomplish overall.

Basically, what we are saying here is that pretty much anyone is able to work with Arduino.

Even if you have the most basic of skills when it comes to coding at all, you will find that this controller is set up for anyone and everyone to learn how to use.

Whether you want to tinker with computer hardware and coding, or you just want to learn a bit of the basics of software and microcomputers, the Arduino system is going to help you to get all of this done.

The Advantages of the Arduino System

The next thing that we need to take a look at here is some of the advantages that will show up when we choose to work with this system over one of the others.

There are a lot of benefits that we can see when it is time to use this system.

This is why there are a lot of programmers, those who are new and even those who have done this programing for some time, who will work with this microcontroller for their own needs.

A few of the advantages and benefits that we are able to see with this controller will include the following:

1. The biggest reason that these kinds of controllers were created in the first place was that they were cost-efficient.

    Rather than $100 or more of other boards, these boards are often going to be less than $50, and the boards that you can manually put together on your own are going to come at an even lower cost.

2. The Arduino environment, or the IDE, is going to work across many different platforms overall.

This means that you can use a computer with Windows on it like any other microcontroller board would require, but you can also work with the Mac operating system computer, or a computer that is going to run with Linux will work as well.

This makes it easier to use any system that you would like while working with the Arduino IDE.

3. The software that you would use with Arduino is going to be considered open-sourced.

   The tools or even the strings of code that you are going to use to instruct the controller on how to behave is something that anyone is able to access.

   You don't have to go through the process of purchasing a license in order to use these tools, making it easier for them to be used in an educational setting.

4. The tools that we are able to get with the Arduino software can be extendable with the C++ libraries and the AVR-C coding language.

   This means that when you have some more in-depth knowledge of these languages, you would be able to expand out the technologies and what they can do more.

5. The environment that you will use to code this controller will be simple and clear to work with.

   You will be able to understand what it is asking you to do and some of the steps that are needed, even if you are brand new to the experience.

   This is going to make working with this software so much easier overall.

6. The hardware is also open-sourced.

   Anyone who has the desire, and the knowledge, would be able to find and even create the hardware that they would like to use along with the Arduino software programming in the environment of the IDE.

   Even those who are not experienced in designing circuits are going to be able to use the breadboard in order to create their own circuit board with Arduino.

As we can see here, there are a lot of benefits that we are able to work with when it comes to using the Arduino system.

And if you are looking for a microcontroller that will be able to get all of your work done in no time and can help you to see some good results in programming and learning along the way, without having to worry about the costs being too high to work with, then this is the right board for us to work with.

What Else Should I Know About Arduino?

Before we get to the end of this chapter and look at a few of the other things that we need to know about Arduino, we need to make sure that we cover a few more topics about this particular system so that we can see why it is so popular to use, and why there are so many programmers, new and old who are trying to learn how to use it.

The number one thing that we have to keep in mind when we are working with Arduino is that it was originally developed with a low-cost point in mind.

The idea was that the other controllers in this market were really expensive to work with, which made them a little bit of a challenge to learn from and try out.

But instead of the Arduino board is $100 or more to work with like the other ones, Arduino is going to be a board that is pre-assembled and comes in around $50.

If you want to be able to learn how to put this together on your own, you can get a board with all of the parts for less.

The IDE, which is also known as the type of environment that we are able to use with Arduino, is going to be nice because it can work with other platforms based on what you are familiar with.

This means that it is not going to be stuck with just the Windows computer, though this is what most of the other microcontrollers are all about on the market, but also with computers that have Linux and Mac on them as well.

This helps the system to appeal to more users because it is going to allow us to use the platform and the operating system that we want.

The third benefit or thing that we need to work with here is that software and how this performs with our Arduino board.

This software is going to be considered open-sourced so that you are able to go through and use it for free.

All of the code strings that you need and are used with this one will help us to tell the controller what you would like it to do, while also being available easily for anyone who would like access to them.

This is going to be an addition that you, as the programmer, will enjoy because you will not have to waste a lot of time purchasing the licensing in order to use the tools as you do with other pieces of technology.

Whether you want to teach some students how to use these programs and the board, or you would like to do some of this kind of training on your own and learn the coding, this is going to be possible with the Arduino board, without having to worry about all of the added costs that come with it.

The open-sourced tools that we just spent our time talking about are going to be pretty easy to extend out if you decide to use the different C++ language and the coding languages that fit under the title of AVR-C.

These are going to be really good libraries to work with that come with all of the additional features that are needed to help you get coding done.

Those who have knowledge of coding and how to use the two general languages that are above, you will find that it is easier to combine these together, as well as their libraries and features, to gain some more knowledge on the board.

There is also going to be quite a bit more when it comes to the depth to the software and the programming features when you decide to use the C language, and a programmer who has some experience and is willing to dedicate more time to this will find that it is easier to accomplish, while being straightforward in the process.

Don't worry if you are a beginner, though.

You will find that these languages will help you to get what you want out of the code without issues.

Another benefit that comes with this one is the environment of Arduino.

This particular controller has an environment that is pretty simple and clear to work with.

This means that the computer program you use and the IDE are going to be able to handle some of the instructions that you are sending over to the controller, and then can turn them over into a form that is easy to handle, and won't require you to have years of experience, or an advanced degree, in order to get done.

This is something that other programmers have run into issues with when they worked with other similar boards, and it could hinder the programming that they want to accomplish.

However, this is not a problem with Arduino, and it will not take that long before you are ready to move forward and really work with this board, even as a beginner.

And finally, we need to have a good idea of how the hardware of this board is going to work.

The good news here is that the hardware is also open-sourced.

The technologies that come with the board will be published under a Creative Commons License which is good because it allows you, while you are doing some of your codings, to make some of the basic changes and modifications that you need to ensure that it works, without any harm being done.

There is just so much that we are able to do when we work with the Arduino technology.

It may seem a bit complicated in the beginning, and it will be too hard to work with or even understand if you haven't been able to work with programming in the past.

But that is part of the beauty that comes with it.

You will find that this is a system and technology that has been designed in order to handle any task that you need, while still being easy for students to learn in the classroom.

Even without a lot of experience in coding and programming, and without a technical background, you will be able to get this down.

And the steps that we talk about in this guidebook will help to make this happen.

Chapter 2: Learning About the Arduino Board

Now that we have some of the basics down about he Arduino board and how it is supposed to work, it is time for us to take a closer look at the actual board and how it is supposed to look.

If you take a glance at this board, it is likely to not make a lot of sense to a beginner in programming, and this can make us feel defeated before we even have a chance to get going.

That is why we are going to spend this chapter learning at least a bit about the Arduino board, the physical board that we are going to spend our time on so that we are able to make it work for our needs before we do the coding.

A Look at the Arduino Board

The very first thing that we need to spend our time on with this is the board itself.

There are going to be a number of parts that naturally come with the board, and we need to have a better idea of what these parts are if we would like to be able to utilize the board along the way.

And we are going to start out with some of the digital pins, which you will notice are all along the edges of your controller.

These are going to be important because they are going to be used to help with the input of our code, or the sensing out of the condition, and they can be there to help with the output as well or the response that your controller should make to the input that it sees.

For example, the input that we want could be something like one of the lights of the sensor going off when it is dark or when it notices that there is a lack of light.

This is going to cause it to close the circuit that is supposed to light up our bulb, and then this is going to be our output.

This is the example that we are going to spend our time on if we want to work with making the board into a nightlight.

On most of the boards that we want to work with, there is also going to be the LED in, which is going to be associated over to the pin that we specify, such as Pin 13 on the Uno of the Arduino.

This is going to be the pin LED that will be there as the only output possibility that we are able to find built into the board, and it is going to be there when we want to create a flashing light later on.

The Pin LED is going to be a great one to work on anytime that you would like to debug or fix some of the code that you have already written, and this will ensure that there aren't any kinds of mistakes that will show up in the process.

The Power LED is going to be just what we can guess from the name.

This is going to be the part that will light up as soon as we see that the board is either turned on or receiving the power that it should.

This is another thing that we are able to set up with some of the codes we work on.

Now, when you take a look at any of the boards that you would like to use, there is going to be the actual part that is known as the microcontroller, which is the ATmega controller.

This is going to be the part that is going to run the whole thing and can be seen as the brains of the project.

It is going to receive all of the instructions that your coding will send to it and then will act out in the manner that it should be based on those codes and instructions.

If you do not take the time to put all of this in place, then the board is going to run into some issues when it is time to function.

Then it is time for us to move on to the part that is going to be all about the analog pins.

In addition to the digital pins that we just did, we need to work with the analog pins, which are going to be found near the edge of our board compared to the digital pins we did.

These are going to be the input that we will be able to find on this kind of system.

When we talk about the analog pins, we are talking about the signal that is going to have some kind of input, but it is not a constant input but one that is able to vary each time.

This could be something that varies like an audio input that is used on the system.

With that example in place, the auditory input in a specific room could change a bit based on who is in the room, how many people are in the room, and other noises that are happening in the background as well.

The 5V and GND pins are going to be another part that we need to focus on because they are used in order to create some additional power of 5V to the circuit and to our microcontroller.

The power connector that comes here is often going to be near the edge that we see with the Arduino board, and it is going to be what we use to provide some power to the microcontroller when it is not plugged back into the USB.

You can find the USB port can be used as our source of power as well, but for the most part, we are going to find that the main function of this is to transfer our upload the set of instructions that we have coded, from the computer where you did the coding, over to the Arduino.

The TX and RX LED"s are going to be used to help us indicate that there is going to be a transfer of information that will occur here.

This indication of communication is what we are going to see when we upload our sketches from our computer to the Arduino so that they are going blink quickly when they are going to do the exchange.

And then we have the reset button is going to make a sound to help reset the controller to its factory settings and erase out any of the information that we have been able to upload to the Arduino.

Other Important Arduino Terms

Another thing that we need to know a bit about when it comes to working on the Arduino system is the types of memory.

There are actually three types that we are able to focus on in this kind of system.

Memory is going to be any of the space where we are able to store the information that is needed to help the system work in the manner that we want.

The first type of memory that we are able to work with is flash memory.

This is where the code for any programs that you write out will be found.

It is going to also go by the name of program space because it is going to be used in an automatic manner for the program when we upload that program to the board.

This type of memory is going to remain in the same place, whether the power is cut off or even when it is time to turn the board off.

The second type of memory that we need to look at is known as the static-random-access memory or SRAM.

This is going to be the space that is found on our controller that the sketch or the program you have created is going to have room to create, store, and do some work with information from the input sources so that you end up with the proper output in the process.

This kind of storage is a bit different because if you do not save the information, it is going to be lost when we lose power to the controller.

EEPROM is going to be similar to a tiny hard-drive that will allow the programmer to store information other than the program itself when we have turned off the board.

There are going to be some separate instructions for this to help out with reading, writing, and erasing, along with some of the other functions that we need to use.

There are going to be certain digital pins that are going to be designated out as PWM pins, meaning that they are going to be there to create an analog with the help of some digital means.

Analog, as we should remember, means that the input or the output is going to be varied, and we are not going to see a constant with this one.

Usually, we are going to see that the digital pins are only going to send out a constant flow of energy.

But when we work with the PWM pins, they are able to vary the pulse of energy that we see between 0 and 5 Volts.

Certain tasks that you are going to try and the program can only be done with these particular pins.

In addition to this, when we are comparing some of the different boards that we are able to do with the Arduino microcontroller, we are going to take a look at the speed of the clock as well.

This is a helpful thing to work with because it tells us more about the speed that we are going to operate our codes at the same time.

The faster speed that we see with this one, the more responsive we get the board to behave as well. keep in mind that this is going to mean that you are using up more battery and more energy in the process.

You have to find the right balance of speed, power, and battery life that works the best for some of your needs.

Another thing that we need to take a look at here is going to be known as the UART.

This is going to be the part that is responsible for measuring out how much serial communication links the device is going to be able to handle along the way.

These lines are going to be the ones that come in and transfer the data in a serial manner, or in a line, rather than sending them out in a parallel manner r simultaneously.

For us to make this one work, we are going to require a lot less hardware compared to other devices, which makes this one so much easier for us to handle overall.

For some of the different projects that we are hoping to focus on with the help of this board, you may need to be able to handle connecting the Arduino to the Internet.

This is why we need to have a few USB drives and more on this device. You will be able to hook up the device and get it to work on any of the different online things that you would like.

There is just so much that we are able to do with the Arduino controller, and being able to learn how to use it and all of the neat things that we are able to do with it can be a lot of fun.

We have gotten through some of the basics to help us get started, but now it is time for us to learn more about what we are able to do with this controller for our own needs.

Chapter 3: Setting Up Our Arduino Board

Now it is time for us to go through and take a look at some of the steps that we need to use in order to actually work with this controller, and when the board is all set up and ready to go, we are able to learn some of the steps that are necessary to get to work.

The first step to all of this, though, is to choose which board, out of the many choices that we would like to work with so let's get started there.

How to Pick Out the Arduino Board to Use

The very first step that we need to use here is to take a look at our choices of boards and then choose which one will work for our projects.

When we are looking through some of the choices that are out there for the boards, there are a few factors that we should consider ahead of time.

One of the factors that are the most important here is how much power we would like this board to have dependent on the applications we want to run.

Of course, if you are just getting started and want to learn a bit of programming without knowing the exact type of project that we want to do, and this means that you may have no idea of the power or the flash memory that you are going to use.

But you will be able to do a little searching and find that there is a big difference between making a simple nightlight and a few of the other simple projects all the way to doing some of the bigger projects like creating our own robotic hand.

Knowing which way you are hoping to go with all of this is going to be important to make sure that you have the power and the memory that you want to work with.

If you think through some of the different parts that you want to accomplish with this ahead of time, you will find that it is a lot easier to figure out which controller options are going to be the best for your needs before you make a purchase.

You have to first look at the amount of power that you would like to have with that board.

When that is determined, it is time to figure out how many of the analog and digital pins you would like to have on the board to get things set up for your projects.

Just like with the other options, you don't necessarily have to be spot on with this, but knowing whether your projects need just a few pins or a lot of them is going to make a big difference in the board that you decide to use in the first place.

If you would like to just use this board to learn a few of the basics of coding and you plan to stick with the simple projects, then you may find that having fewer of these pins is going to be just fine.

But, if you plan to grow into the board, or you want to jump right in and take on a lot of the more complicated parts along the way, then you need to make sure that you go with a board that has a lot more pins to get it all done.

This is going to require you to have a few more ideas of what your goals are in order to get it done.

The next thing on the list that we need to spend some time on is whether we would like to work with one of these controllers that are wearable or not.

This is going to be a personal decision based on what you are doing with the project, but it is a choice you can make when you pick out your devices, so it is important to consider as well.

This is something that we talked about earlier in this guidebook, but we need to consider ahead of time whether we would like to see the Arduino controller connect back to the internet or not.

If you would like to have that ability to connect to the internet, then you will need to look for that feature when choosing aboard.

Keep in mind that while a lot of these controllers come with this capability, this doesn't always ring true, so think it through ahead of time too.

Picking out the board that you would like to use is not always as easy as it seems.

It takes a lot of time, and it can be a challenge because there are a lot of choices for you to pick from.

Knowing how many pins you want, the power that should be behind the device and more, are all going to be important based on what you are looking for in the process.

How to Use the Arduino IDE

Once you have had a chance to look over the different Arduino boards that you want to use, it is time to learn more about the IDE, or the environment, that works with this.

The software that we want to create or run in this controller has to be useable on the IDE, or it won't work.

This means that we need to take the time to either download the desktop IDE to do the code, or we can find an online version of the IDE and do some of the codings in that.

The first thing that we may want to try out with this IDE is to do a few of the codes, but we need to make sure that we are able to download the application, using the format that works the best with our own desktop computer.

There are a few options that you can choose from, which opens up the possibilities based on your own program as well.

First, there is a desktop application that works well with the Windows system.

This one allows you to do it from the tablet or phone along with a computer or desktop that relies on Windows to make things easier if you choose.

However, this is not the only version of the IDE that you are able to work with, which is one of the benefits of working with the Arduino system rather than one of the other controllers.

You can also find that this IDE is going to work with the Mac OS X as well if you choose to do this.

It is not going to work on the Apple mobile devices, though, so keep this in mind; it does work well on laptops and desktops with this system on it.

In addition, you are able to use this IDE on the Linux operating system as well.

It works with a few of the different distributions that come with that, which will open up more opportunities based on what you are trying to get done in the process.

You can use the option that is on the web to help you work directly with the Arduino IDE, or it comes with the 32-bit and the 64-bit options as well.

When you are ready to get started with all of this, you need to make sure that you are going through and downloading the version of the desktop IDE that you are hoping to use.

You are the ability to run the application that you need for installation, click through some of the different options that are there, and before any time at all has passed, you will have the Arduino IDE up and running for your own needs.

This is going to be a helpful step to work with because it is going to make it easier for the programmer to have access to the IDE and to some of the other software that we want to work with when it comes to these processes.

You are also able to run it from different sources if you want, based on the kinds of projects that you would like to complete.

How to Code Your Programs in Arduino

The net step in this process is that we want to be able to take our programs and write some codes on the controller we are using.

We will look at the specific codes that we can write with these later, but for now, we are going to spend some time learning more about how to understand how to write the codes specifically on our IDE so that it performs the application that we want in the process.

Writing code does not have to be all that difficult, so don't let that scare you away if you are new to the world of coding.

There are a number of different coding languages that you can use for this one, so it can be as simple as you need it to be.

The IDE is going to be the part of our controller that will make creating codes and executing them as simple as possible, which is why we took some time to learn how to use it.

Once we have been able to do some practicing to write out codes, we then need to make sure that there is a way to execute and run the code, and then, if some issues show up, we can ensure that we are able to troubleshoot them as soon as they show up.

You will find that the best way to do this is to apply the programs that you want to code onto the controller, and then see whether or not it is able to run or not.

We first need to connect to the board, which is the next step in our process here.

How to Connect to the Arduino Board

Now, when we take a look at some of the options that we have on boards, you may notice that many of them are going to come with a port for a USB drive in them.

To get started with connecting the board then, we need just to take the right ends of the USB cord and plug it into our computer and into the Arduino board that we are using.

This will get the Arduino board hooked up to the part of the computer that we want.

When we are able to do all of this, you will find that the software that comes with the IDE for our Arduino will instantly start to recognize the type of board that you are trying to use.

If this is not something that happens, then we just have to go through and choose which board is the correct one from the dropdown menu on the screen.

In addition to using the USB that we just talked about, we may need to bring out, in some situations, the TKDI cable, or a breakout board to help make sure that our controller is going to be completely compatible with the computer we are currently using.

This process is going to involve us going through and inserting the TKDI into the right board on the controller, similar to what we did with the USB.

For the most part, though, the USB is going to work just fine for our needs, and we can just rely on that part to get everything done.

How to Upload the Arduino Board

To help us get some of the work done that we need for uploading the sketch and the code that was already created, you have to take the time to go through and pick out the right port and the right board that you would like to see this uploaded to.

It should be a simple process to go through and pick out the board that we want to use because you just need to look at the titles of the board and then match it up to the ones that show up for you.

To help us make sure that w are selecting out the right serial port for this, we do get to choose from a number of options to make this work, including some of the following:

For a Mac computer, we are going to have two options.

If we are working with Leonardo, Mega2560, or Uno, we are going to use the code below:

/dev/tty.usbmodem241

But if you are working with the boards that are Deumilanove or some of them even earlier boards, you will use the code below:

/deve/tty.usbserial-1B1

For all of the other options that are going to be connected with the adapter that works from USB to serial, you would work with the following option:

/dev/tty.USA19QW1b1P1.1

Then we are able to move on to working with a Windows operating system and how this will work for some of our needs.

If we are working with a serial board, we are going to work with either COM1 or COM2.

If you are working with a board that is connected to a USB, you will want to work with COM4, COM5, or COM7 or higher.

You should look inside of your Windows Device Manager to help you to determine which port on that board or device that you are using and then go from there.

Then we can also work with the Linux system as well.

If you are going to hook it up with a serial port, you will use the code below:

/dev/tty.ACMx

If you would like to use the board for something like a USB port, you would need to use the code:

/dev/tty.USBx.

Once we have been able to actually use these codes and select the right board and port for our needs, it is then time to click on the button for Upload before we choose which of the Sketches is the best one from the menu that shows up.

One thing to remember here is that if you are working with a board that is a bit newer, you will find that the process of uploading a sketch is easy, but some of the older boards need to go through a reset or some other work in order to get the sketch to work properly.

Running the New Program in Arduino

At this point, we are ready for the main event.

We need to look at some of the steps that are needed to run the software in Arduino with that program that we wrote above.

The good news here is that there are a few methods that we are able to use to help us add in some power to the board of Arduino once the code is all programmed onto it.

The first method that we will use is to power all of this with that USB connection that we installed earlier on.

You can just hook the controller to your computer, and you are ready to go.

The second method is to use the ethernet cord and hook it up to this manner by using it with the necessary network.

And the third method that we can use is to just add in some battery power and let it run in this manner.

Once you have been able to get that power-up and connected so that you can use it, you have the right input in, and you have added the software, then it will all be done.

This is the point where everything is going to perform the function that it should and you are ready to do some programming and more with the help of your own Arduino microcontroller.

Chapter 4: How Coding Works With Arduino

We spent a little bit of time taking a look at how the coding is supposed to work with Arduino in the last chapter, but we are going to dive into some of the codings a little bit more to ensure that even a beginner is on the right track to making this all work for their needs.

Coding a program with the Arduino controller means that we will need to go through and write out our programs using one of the various coding languages that are out there.

If this sounds a bit scary to you as a beginner, the good news is that it is not as hard as you may think, and there are a number of different languages that you can choose from that are designed for the Arduino, and designed to be easier for beginners to learn how to use.

In the same manner that we are going to see the study of mathematics has its own sets of symbols that are going to denote some of the different functions that we are meant to do, like addition and multiplication, we will find that there are a number of symbols and terms that we need to know in order to get started with coding.

If you have spent some time working with any coding language in the past, then you should find that the language with Arduino is going to be simple to learn.

Even if you have never worked with coding in the past and you are not sure what you are doing, the language of Arduino is not hard and you will be able to figure it all out fairly quickly.

Let's get started and learn a bit more about how we can work with coding in the Arduino microcontroller.

The Structure

The first part of this is how to set up some of the structure that needs to be found in this kind of coding language.

We will start out with the setup() method.

This is the function that we are going to call out when the sketch starts.

And it is only going to run one time after we do the startup or when we reset the board.

You are able to use it for several different things, such as starting variables, pin modes, or for use with some of the libraries.

There are also a few other terms that we are able to use when it is time to add in the extra functionality that we need.

Then we need to work with the loop(). The loop function will require this controller board to go through and repeat the function that you set up more than one time.

It can go on continuously until a certain condition or variable is that you set is actually met.

We are going to set the condition so that it is going to stop the loop, or you will essentially freeze up the program that you are working with, and you will need to turn the board off to get it to stop.

The Control Structures

Now that we have some of the information about the structure set up and ready to go, it is time for us to take a little look at some of the control structures.

These control structures are going to be important to note because they are going to show us the manner in which we are going to be able to take in the input.

Just like we are able to guess with a name, there are going to be a variety of inputs regarding control that we are able to use to help us determine how the readout for our data should be.

Another thing that is considered in this is known as the provisional language.

This provisional language is considered at the time of analyzing our data, so we know which output needs to happen at which time.

All of the languages that work with Arduino have to follow this, so let's take a look at a few of these.

The first option that we are going to explore is known as the if statement.

This is the first conditional statement, and it is going to be one that is simple and not used that much because of some of its limitations.

This is going to be a useful option to help us link together a condition or one of the inputs to the chosen output that we set up.

It means that if a certain condition that we set are met, then a specific output or response from the controller is going to happen.

Let's say that we are working with a thermometer here.

If we have this attached to our Arduino controller and it gets higher than 75 degrees at a time, you could set up the code to tell the board that it should send a signal to your air conditioner so that it will turn on, thereby decreasing the temperature to get it back to the 75 degrees and no higher at the time.

If it stays at 75 degrees or less, then nothing is going to happen when if the statement is in use.

Then it is time for us to move onto the second conditional statement, which is known as the if else statement.

This is going to be similar to the conditional if statement that we did above, but instead, it is going to tell another kind of action that our controller is able to take if the first condition is not met in the process.

This is a good one to use because it will make sure that a potential two actions are going to happen based on what is going to happen along the way.

After we work with the conditional statements, it is time for us to move on to some of the loops.

The while loop is the first option that we are able to use is the while loop.

This is going to be the one that will be able to continue on in an indefinite manner until the condition that you set up is seen to be false again.

What this is going to mean for some of our codings is that this loop is going to perform a certain function until the parameters that you set are no longer being met, and then the statement that will be ruling over the condition that you made is false.

Then the loop is done.

The second loop that we are able to work with is known as the do while loop, and it is similar to the while statement.

However, you will find that it is going to make sure that the condition is going to be checked one time, before the loop is ever tested out with the variable, rather than having this happen at the beginning of things.

When we are focusing on some of the loops, we need to make sure that there is some kind of break function that is showing up.

This is going to be the exit point of the loop and will ensure that the controller will not get stuck in an endless loop while it is doing its work.

Always double-check to make sure that you are doing this one well, or you are going to end up with a mess with your code.

Another thing to take a look at is known as the return function.

This return function is a great way to make sure that we are able to send one of our functions, and if it end sup returning to us some kind of value when the function is terminated, then we end up with the calling function or the function that is asking for that kind of information in the first place.

The way this goes depends on the type of codes we are writing.

The last thing that we need to look at is the "goto" function.

This is going to be a useful function that is going to tell our Arduino controller that it needs to move over to another place, any place that is not consecutive in the coded program.

It is going to transfer some of the flow over to one of the other parts of the program, and it is going to be discouraged in some cases by other programmers of the C language, but it can be useful to simplify some of the programs that we want to create with this controller.

The Coding Syntax

We now need to take a look at some of the syntax that we are able to create when it comes to coding in the Arduino board.

There are a few parts of this syntax that we are able to work with and need to spend our time on.

Knowing these parts are going to ensure that we get the best results in the process.

Some of the syntax parts that we need to focus our attention on here will include:

1. The semicolon:

    This is going to be used as a type of period in the English language because it helps us to end the statement we are using in coding.

    We have to make sure that the statement we are closing up with the semicolon is one that we consider complete, or we will find that the code will not work out in the right manner along the way.

2. Curly braces:

These are going to be useful and have a lot of complex functions in our codes, but the main thing that we need to know at this point is that when they are inserted in the beginning, you do need to follow all of that up with a pair of curly braces to get it closed up.

This is going to make sure that the information in the braces is balanced and will not allow someone else to mess around with them.

3. // or a single line comment:

If you would like to set a reminder for yourself or to tell another person about how the code is going to function, then we need to use this code to begin the comment.

Make sure that with this one that we are only taking up one line at a time.

This is not going to transfer over to the processor of your controller, but will be live in the code, and can be a good reference to you, as well as to anyone else who is manually going through the code:

4. /* */ or a multi-line comment:

This type of comment is going to open up and can span past more than one line.

It is going to contain just a single line comment but is not going to contain another multi-line comment as well.

Be sure to close with the other part of the process, or the whole of the code that comes after this is going to be seen as a comment and it won't be implemented for you.

5. #define:

This is going to be the part that will ensure that we are able to define a certain variable as a value that is more constant.

It is going to provide us a name to value as a shorthand method for that value.

These are not going to end up with any memory space used on the chip, so it is great to use them as a way to conserve the space that we have on the compiler.

6. #include:

This is going to be the one that we are able to use when we would like to add in a few more libraries to any sketch that we are trying to use, such as including other words and other coding languages to the sketch, ones that re not automatically found there.

For example, if you are going through this, you could decide to include the C or the AVR libraries and some other tools to make the coding easier, and this is going to help get it done.

a. One main thing that we need to remember with this one is that you do not want to add in a semicolon to the end of this statement, and the same rule is going to apply when you work with the #define that we talked about before.

If we do add this semicolon at this point to close things up, then you will end up with an error here, and the code is not going to work well.

The Different Types of Data

Now that we know a bit more about the topics above, it is time for us to look at some of the different data types that can be found with all of this.

The data types that we are talking about here are going to refer to some of the types of data that can be handled by the different setups of programming that we want to apply.

The data that you can receive through this system is going to be sent over to the program that you would like to choose to help determine the outcomes as well.

There are a lot of options when it comes to the types of data that we want to use, but some of the most common will include:

1. Void:

   This is going to be the function that we are going to use to help tell the controller that you are not wanting it to send back any information when the function is done.

2. Boolean:

   This is going to be a data type that holds onto two values.

   It will either be true or false.

This is going to be available to use with any of the functions that you want to rely on.

The function is going to return something that is true here or something that is false, based on the input and the kinds of conditions that you put in place.

3. Char:

This is going to be a type of character that we are able to find in your code, such as a single letter.

It can also be a numeric character as well.

You are often going to work with strings of characters to form the words and sentences that you need as well.

4. Unsigned char:

This is going to be similar to what we find with the characters that we talked about above, but we are going to focus more on numbers, going from 0 to 255 to help signify characters rather than the signed characters, which have the potential to include something that is negative.

5. Byte:

This is going to be a data type that we can work with that will help us to store a number.

It can also go from 0 to 255 but will be an 8-bit system of binary numbers.

6. Int:

   This is going to b the integers that you are able to use and will be one of the main methods that you are able to use to store some of the numbers that you would like to work with.

7. Word:

   When we talk about the word data type, it is going to store up to 16-bit unsigned numbers on the Uno and on other boards that you would like to work with.

   When you work with the part known as Due or Zero, you are going to work with numbers that are 32-bit with the help of some words.

   This is basically going to be one of the main ways that we are able to store the integers and numbers.

8. Float:

This is going to be one of the number types that is going to count as single-digit that will then be followed with decimal points, up to seven of them, and then it can be multiplied by ten up to the power of 38 if you need one that goes this big.

You can then use this to store some of the more precise numbers, or at least a few that are a bit bigger.

These are going to handle a lot of processing power, and they only come up with 7 decimal points here, so it may not be what you need for everything.

9. Double:

This is going to be a data type that is really only relevant when we want to work with the type known as Due, which is going to allow us time to get double precision to our float number.

For all of the other boards and controllers that come with Arduino, this is not something that we want to use often, but it can help us increase our precision or our accuracy as well.

As we can see with all of this, this is going to be some of the basics that we must learn about when it comes to the Arduino controller and the languages that are going to help us get it all set up and ready to go.

Learning some of these basics and what we are really able to do with them in the process will make it so much easier for us to get everything out of this device controller that we need.

Chapter 5: How to Turn the Arduino Into a Personal Machine

Once we are able to learn a little bit about the coding that needs to happen with the Arduino controller, it is time for us to learn a bit more about putting this to work and actually turning it into the personal machine that we want to use.

While the switches and the buttons that are found with this kind of board are going to be easy to work with and open up a lot of possibilities, there is still going to be a lot more that we can do with this board other than turning it on and off.

Although Arduino is going to be known as a digital device, it is going to help us sometimes receive the information that we need from an analog sensor so that it is able to measure a lot of things in the environment around us, like measuring out the temperature and figuring out if there is light on or not.

There are also some different options for the programming languages and inputs that we want to use to provide us with the right results so that the outputs we get often depend on the sensors and the coding that you choose.

You are going to find that a lot of these sensors and what they mean can be found on the official website for Arduino.

To create all of this, though, we would need to use the built Analog to Digital Converter with Arduino.

You will then be able to use a temperature sensor in this instance to help determine something like the warmth of your skin.

This is going to be a device that we can figure out by using a changing voltage that is there based on what is detected.

To make all of this work for us, we are going to work with a total of three pins on our board.

The first pin is going to be our grounding pin, and then the other will connect to the power source that we want to use.

And then we need that third pin is going to be the one that helps to transfer the voltage of the variable over to our controller.

This particular project is also going to come with its own sketch that is going to ensure that we are able to interpret with the sensor, and ten will turn on the LED that is there, then turns it off again, displaying for us the warmth level that is going to be there.

The temperature setting and the sensors are going to be provided back to us with different types.

For example, the TMP36 is going to be the one that we will focus our attention on for this project because it is going to show us a new voltage that will be different other than what shows up with the Celsius measurement as well.

This can help us to see the temperature in a format that we are used to working with.

Keep in mind with this one that the IDE that comes with this controller is going to feature a serial monitor device.

This device is going to allow us a way to record some of the results that come out of that controller.

When we use this serial monitor, it is going to make it easier to discover some of the information that will relate to the status of the sensors and can make it so that we learn about the circuit and some of the code that must be run to get this particular program to work for us.

How to Create Our Circuit

With some of that background in place, it is time for us to take a look at our first step, which is going to include creating the circuit.

Now, we are going to work through this process and work with this in a manual manner, but we are going to work on calibrating it to make this work.

We are going to use the button that will help to provide the reference temperature or let the Arduino controller go before the loop starts, and then have that as our reference part on this, so we know where to work from.

To make this happen, we need to work with a few of the following steps:

1. First, we need to connect the breadboard that we are using to the ground.

2. Then connect the cathode of every LED that we have to the ground with the help of the resistor.

   Join the anodes of the LEDs to pins 2 using 4. These are important because they are going to be the indicators of the project.

From there, we want to be able to position the TMP26 to the breadboard by letting the rounded part face away from the board that you are using.

Then you need to joint he flat facing side of the left pin to the power, and then the right pin over to the ground.

We can then connect the central pin over to the AO on the Arduino we are working with.

The next step that we want to focus on is building up an interface for the sensor that will make it easier for the users to work with it.

You can even work with a cutout of paper that is going to resemble the human hand if this helps you to get this done.

If you are right with it, you are able to build up a pair of lips for a person to kiss, and then note how this is going to look.

You might also need to spend some time to mark out the LED's so that you can get the meaning out of them.

To keep going with this, we want to bring out some paper and then do some cutting so that this is able to fit right on top of our breadboard.

We are then able to create some of the lips where the sensors should be placed.

We need to make sure that when we do this, there are a few circles so that we can see through with the LEDs.

From there, we are going to cover up some of the cutouts of the lips on the breadboard so that the lips are going to still surround the sensor and the LEDs in the holes.

Then you can press down on this in order to see how this feels.

When we get to this part, it is going to be time for us to examine our coding a bit to make sure that it is going to work well.

What Are Some of the Useful Constants?

Constants are going to be important to what we are focusing our attention on here, and it will not take long for you to find that they come with some unique names so that you are able to find them and use them in the proper manner.

This is going to be pretty similar to variables that are used in other coding languages, but they are not changeable at all.

We need to spend some time assigning a name to the analog input so that they are easier to reference, and then we can create the instance that is unique that will help us to store the temperature that we would like to work with as the reference.

For every degree that we find to pass on as part of the reference temperature, then the LED is going to turn itself on.

The temperature is going to be written out, and then it is going to be stored as a floating-point number.

This is going to be the only part of the process that is able to hold onto the one decimal point that we need overall.

When we get to the following step, we are going to work with what is known as the initialization of our serial port.

When we work with this one, we are going to learn how to interact with a brand new command, which is going to be known here as Serialbegin().

This command is going to be important because it is going to help us start up a connection between the computer and the board as well.

This is the link that will help us to read over the values to form the analog input onto the screen of the computer.

The argument that we are going to see here is there to represent the speed of communication that will start with Arduino.

You can then go through and use the serial monitor of the IDE that is here with it to make it easier to observe all of the information that is picked out, and then you can send this out from the controller you are working with.

From this point, we are going to work on making sure the digital pin is initialized, and then we can switch it to turn off at the right time.

This is going to be a useful thing to work with when we set up the for loop, which is easy to turn on just a few pins out of the output.

These are going to be the pins where we get contact with our LEDs to start with.

Instead of taking the time to assign each of then unique names to these pins and using the function known as pinMode(), you can use them in a loop to make it easier because it is more efficient to get the work done.

This is a good trick to use if you would like to get things to repeat a bunch of times without having to waste space and try to get them to match up.

At some point in this process, we want to be able to get the sensor to show up with the right temperature, and then we can read out that output as well.

While the loop is proceeding from above, we want to make sure that we are working with a new variable, which we will call sensorVal in order to hold onto the reading from the sensor for us.

If you want to take the time to read this sensor, you just need to go through and call up the function of analogRead(), which will then be able to accept a single argument.

Keep in mind here that this is not the only thing that we need to work on here.

We need also to take some time to go through and transfer the value of the sensor over to the computer that is connected.

The function that we see with Serial.print() is going to be used to help us gather up all of the data out of the sensors that are on the Arduino controller and then will move it over to the PC of your choice.

You can then use your serial monitor to help you to check out the information when you want.

If you have taken some time to go through these steps and you assigned the parameter for Serial.print() in the quotation marks, it is then going to be something that will show up in the text that we typed up.

In addition, if you decide that you are going to work with the variable as your parameter for this, then this will show up as the value of the variable right from the start.

Then it is time for us to go through and convert the sensor reading into a voltage.

With some knowledge of math, you are able to go through and determine the right pin voltage that you want to work with.

The voltage can range from 0 to 5 volts and has some fractions that are going to show us as well.

It is important to remember that you will need to go through and declare a float variable in order to get it stored where you would like.

From here, it is time for us to go through and change over the voltage to a good temperature before it gets all loaded up onto our computer.

The sheet of data that we are going to see with this sensor is going to have a ton of information on it, information that is similar to what we are going to see when we talk about the voltage of the output.

The sheets of data are simply going to be our electronic manuals.

They are usually created by engineers, and they are done in a manner that helps other engineers in the process.

Based on the data that we are going to get from the sensors, every ten millivolts is going to be about one degree of change in Celsius.

In addition, we will then be able to go through and define what we want to use as the offset for the values when we get below the freezing point.

So, if we are working with minus 05 from the voltage, and then you can multiply this by 100, you will be able to get the actual temperature that we want to work with.

Now, if we are doing this process and we find that we get a lower temperature, then you may want to set this up so that the LEDs will turn off.

When you work with the starting temperature that we chose, it is possible to define the if else statement to help the program know when to turn on the light, and when to turn it off.

By using this as the reference temperature and a good point to work with, you can switch on the LED lights after you see a change of just 2 degrees in temperature.

Then the program is set up in order to scan through for a range of values as we look through the scale of our temperatures.

When this is done, the next part of the process that we want to work with is turning on the LED in order to create a lower temperature.

The && operator is going to stand for "and" in the more logical sense and can help us with this.

This is going to work in a manner that allows us to check out whether or not there are multiple conditions that are happening with this process in the first place.

Then we can change things around and work through a process that allows us to have a medium temperature that is going to turn on two of our LED lights when we want them to.

Then, when the sensor notices that the temperature has fallen down a bit, somewhere between two and four degrees above or below the baseline based on what we want to do, then the block of code is going to turn on the LED, and this is going to show up in pin 3.

Of course, this is just one of the examples that we can use when it comes to working with a variety of codings that we are able to do with the Arduino language.

And when we can combine all of this together with some of the coding basics and the information that is present in the C language, which we will talk about in a little bit, then you can definitely add in a bit more functionality to what we are looking for in this board.

Chapter 6: The C Language

Now that we have had a chance to take a look at how the Arduino language is going to look, we are going to take this to another level and look a bit more at the C language.

This is one of the best options to use when it comes to working on the Arduino board, and it is worth our time to work with this one and learn some of the basics that happen with it.

You will find that as you go through working on this language, that it is going to be parts that you can work with that may be a bit confusing and not make all that much sense until you actually run the program, which is going to take it a bit harder for us to work with compared to other languages.

But the instruments that are going to work out well on this kind of controllers, such as the sensors and the LEDs, are going to depend on the specific outputs and inputs that we will work on here.

And many of the different programming languages that we can find online and more can handle the work that we want to do with the Arduino board, but you will find that the C language is often seen as the best, and that is the one that we will focus on here.

A primary system for any kind of technology that we want to work with is going to consist of what is known as the control device, which is going to refer back to the CPU or the actual microcontroller that we were spending some time talking about before.

There are also going to be a few differences that are going to show up when we pick a specific controller to work with as well.

But, keep in mind that these controllers are not going to be as powerful compared to what we see with a standard microprocessor.

It is still going to contain the input, the output ports, and the hardware functions that we want.

You will find here that the microprocessors that we are talking about are going to be connected back to the external memory.

Generally, the controllers are going to contain the right amount of memory onboard.

However, when we say this, we are not really talking about the larger sizes.

It is possible for the controller that we are using with Arduino to have only a few hundred bytes or so of memory for some of the simple applications that it uses.

The register is going to be the only place where we are able to have logical-mathematical operations that we would like to carry out.

For example, if you would like to carry out an example of the addition of two variables, the value of these variables is something that we are going to need to move over to the register.

There are many benefits to working with the C language, and it is important that we learn how to use it properly.

It is similar to a lot of the work that we have done with the Arduino language, and we will look at a few of the different options that we are able to do with it along the way in this guidebook as well.

Before we dive into that though, we need to take a look at some more of the basics that will come with this language, and in particular, we are going to take a look at a concept that is known as the memory maps and how this is going to help C get the most out of our Arduino boards.

The Memory Maps

Each memory byte that is going to show up on our computer system will come with their own address connected to them.

Now, if this address is not actually in place, then the process is going to run into trouble because it has lost its means to identify the memory that we are hoping to get in contact with.

To keep it simple, you will often find that the memory address is going to start out with zero and then can increase and go up in memory from there, even though there is the potential for a particular address to be more specific or follow a system that is more unique.

It is also possible in some cases that the address that you are looking for may not point to the output or the input port at all when it is time to work with external communication.

For the most part when we are working on this kind of language, and some of the communication that you want to handle here, it is going to be a necessity for us to go through and do a memory map to see the location and the state of the memory on our system.

This is going to be a big undertaking and it is going to leave us with a massive array of the slots of memory that we have to work with along the way.

Those who spend their time looking through these maps know that it can take some time, and they need to spend at least some of their time working with the address with the least value positions at the top while the others who draw the map and assign the last address to the bottom will be there in this as well.

You will find that each of the points of the address will tell us a place where we are able to store some more bytes inside of the memory of our computer as well.

As we go through the following chapters of this guidebook, you will notice that we are going to spend a good deal of time looking through some of the basics of the C language.

There are many languages that work well with the Arduino board, but none of them are going to provide us with the power and some of the functionality to this controller like we are going to find with the C language.

If you already know one of these other languages, then feel free to add those into the mix and use them instead.

However, if you are a beginner in coding and programming at all, then we are going to spend some more time through this guidebook, looking at the basics of the C language and all of the cool things that you will be able to do with it.

Some of the basics that we will talk about will work specifically with the Arduino board and what we are able to do with it here.

And this can help you to actually begin using this microcontroller for some of your own projects early on.

Chapter 7: The Logic Statements

Now that we have had some time to work with the C language and at least discuss why it is a good language for us to explore and work with when it comes to this board, it is time to move on to some of the logic statements in this language, and how they are going to bring us forward when we are doing some of our work in this kind of process.

The first circuit that we took some time to talk about before was meant to be pretty basic because it was there to make the process of working on these as easy as possible.

But it is time for us to go through and change things up.

When it is time for us to go through and work on some programming with our controller where the input is actually going to have some kind of effect on the output, then it is time to work with a process in coding known as the logic statements.

These logic statements are important in our coding, whether we use the C language or not because they are one of the best ways for the programmer to come in and check that the value of the variable is going to be compared to some of the other values that we have.

This other value is going to depend on what we are hoping to compare in our own codes, but it is possible to be either a fixed object, or it could be a variable.

When we use these logical statements, it is going to be one of the methods that the programmer uses in order to gain as much control as possible over what is going to happen in some of their sketches, without the programmer being able to guess what is going to happen next ahead of time.

To help us to follow along with making some of our own logic statements, we need to go into the IDE of the Arduino and then work with a specific path.

The path that works well here is going to be File, Examples, 02. Digiatl, Button.

Take a moment here to notice how similar the code that we just did above, or the path, is to some of the other codes that we have written out in this guidebook so far.

You can tell that this is a similar pattern that is used with these controllers, which is going to make them all that much easier to use as time goes on.

Now, we need to look a bit closer at some of the variables, and the one that is the most important for us right now is going to be the pin of the button, and then the other is going to be more about the state of the button.

This can tell us whether or not our button is on.

When we were in the setup mode, we are going to work with the pinMode to make sure that the pins will be initialized as we go.

But for the situation we are in now, we are going to have the button pin with the direction of INPUT, which is going to tell the chip that the current should head on in, rather than heading out.

At this point, when we work with this kind of loop, we are going to actually get into our program, and then the very first line that is there will be able to introduce another function to make sure that we can get things done.

In this, we will be able to work with the coding of digitalRead(), which is going to be the counterpart that comes with the command of digitalWrite() that we looked at earlier on.

This is also a good place to look to when we want to see how these Boolean codes are supposed to work as well.

This is going to mean the logical statements, and now it is time for us to get a bit more into these.

The outcome that we are able to see with this one is really going to depend on whether or not there are specific kinds of conditions that are met.

The command is already going to be great here because it goes through the perfect condition for this part of the code, and this is something that we will hear about ahead of time.

While we are here, we also need to go through and check out the button state and whether this has been pressed.

When the button has been pressed, it is going to show us the result of HIGH.

The expression is an if statement here, and this is going to be the piece of code that will show up and work inside of our curly braces in the code.

This is going to make it easier for us to know whether it is going to behave the way that we want.

Next, we are going to see an else statement that will come with some curly braces to work with as well.

else means that if the input is pushed to the statement and it doesn't meet up with the first statement, then it is going to head over to the part of the code in the curly braces and work with that part instead.

In the example that we are working with here, this is again going to work with the digitalWrite() part of the code to help tell the chip on the Arduino board that it is time to turn or light of just like we did earlier.

One thing that we need to remember when we are doing this is while the sketch is going to come with the else statement, it is not required to have this with all of the sketches we work with, and sometimes we can just work with the if statement without needing to work with the if else statement.

Instead, it is possible to set it up so that when our specific condition is not met, then the code will not go through and run the next set of instructions at all. In some programs, this will work just fine.

With all of this information in mind, it is time to look a bit closer at how we can take our controller and get it to blink the LED light just when we push on one of the buttons.

There are also a few simple circuits that are easy to choose from on this controller, but then we need to take a few moments in order to figure out how to work with each one.

To help us get through this project and see what needs to happen with it, we need to open up the following:

File → Examples → of.Control → WhileStatementConditional

The first part that we are going to be able to get out of this sketch is something that should look pretty familiar to what you are doing.

We are going to go through and declare the variables that we are going to need, initializing them, and then setting the pins to help correct the settings which are going to be either the output or the input.

Once we hit the main loop that comes with the program, we are then going to be able to get a bit of experience with what our while statement is going to look like. Some of the code that we need to work with this includes:

```
while (digitalRead(buttonPin) == HIGH( {

        calibrate();
```

This statement is actually going to provide us with a lot of information, even though it is small and doesn't look like there is a ton in it.

Because it is so small, we need to actually divide it up so that we can see what all is found inside.

The first thing to look at here is the while statements.

These are important as long as we add something into the curly braces so that we can set up our conditions.

This brings us to the condition that is going to show up at the beginning of that code.

If the button is pressed and we will call that our condition, we then need to go through and check the pin that is supposed to be associated with this button to see if it is pressed or high.

If this is true, ten is going to be able to calibrate, which is a function that the user can go through and define later.

What this is going to mean in this code is that when the program sees that you have a command to go through and calibrate, it is going to jump on over to the instructions that you originally set for that function.

It can then execute them before heading back to that part of the code.

We can also spend a bit of time looking at this particular function since this is what is being called at the time.

We are going to take a look at the void calibrate() } part of the code.

At the beginning here, it is going to look familiar because it is going to be similar to the loop() and the setup() functions that we were using already.

What this line of code is going to tell the compiler is that you would like to be able to define a function with the name of calibrating, and then it is going to return the void to you, which shows no argument.

This brings us to the part where we are going to try and figure out what all of this means.

First, we are going to take the time to see that defining the calibration means that if we go through and type in the same word into the code in a new part then the compiler is going to spend some time searching for a function that comes with the same name, and it wills till running in a manner similar to what we are doing now.

But what happens when we get a return of void?

We haven't really had much of a chance to talk about the return of a void, because our goal here is just to assume that the loop is going to work and will return us with something.

This particular function is one that does work, but it is not always going to be the case when we add in the void work.

Any time that the function can go through and complete any and all of the instructions that are in our braces, it is going to provide us with a value of the function.

This can be in many forms, including a void or no return, but it is possible that it could be an integer or another type of number that goes with the calculations that we want to work with.

To make this easier and to see what more we are able to do here, let's say that we are working with a function.

Instead of going through and figuring out the weekly earnings of those who work for company A, we will change it up and get the function to handle floating numbers that will contain all of the values of those earnings so that we can use them in a new place in our program.

If this is what we want to work with, which function should we choose?

This is a good way to help us think about how we are going to use our functions, and the logical statements to work for our particular projects.

As we can imagine already, there are a wide variety of different logical expressions that we can bring out for the Arduino language, and all of them are going to come with different purposes along the way.

These may seem like complex to work within the beginning, but they are going to make a big difference in the results that you are able to get with your board and can ensure that the controller is able to function properly based on the input and output, and the different conditions that you decide to set along the way.

Chapter 8: Operators to Use on the Arduino Board

When it comes to using the C language, it is important to spend at least a little bit of time looking at some of the operators that are usable in this language.

There are operators in all of the coding languages that you may want to spend your time on, and while these seem like really basic parts of the coding, they are going to be important to some of the work that you want to get done.

They are small but powerful, and without them, you will not be able to get your code to work.

These operators, in the C language and in other languages, are simply just symbols that are going to be used to help us to perform operations for getting things done as much as possible.

The operators that we are going to use when we focus on this language can include options like logical, bitwise, and arithmetic along with Boolean.

While all of these are important, and there are other operators that we are able to focus on, we are going to narrow it down to the two that you are most likely to find when working on your own Arduino controller, the arithmetic and the Boolean operators.

Let's dive in and see how this one will work.

The Arithmetic Operators

The first type of operator that we are able to work on here is going to be the arithmetic operators.

These are going to be the operators that we want to focus on in order to handle our own mathematical operations that we have.

If you are doing code and you need to add in or subtract two numbers (or more) from one another, then these arithmetic operators are going to be able to help.

The arithmetic operators are going to include addition, subtraction, multiplication, and dividing part of the code based on what you would like to see happen with the various numbers in the code.

It is even possible to have more than one of the arithmetic operators show up in one part of the code that you are working with, and you can even have multiples show up in the same line.

We simply have to remember that we must work with the idea of the order of operations.

This ensures that we are able to go through and get the mathematics done well and that we will end up with the right answers along the way.

The Boolean Operators

Another option that we are able to work within this language is going to be some of the Boolean operators.

These are going to be based on the idea that the output you are going to get will either be true or false.

There are going to be a few different options that we are able to work with when we are in the Arduino system, including &&, || and !.

These are the two main types of operators that you will want to focus on when working on this kind of board and making it work for some of the results that you are looking for in the process.

Learning how to make these happen, and ensuring that you are able to get them to show up in the codes in the right manner, and at the right time, will be important to the overall coding we are doing.

Chapter 9: Computer Interfacing

It is now time for us to go through and do some of the necessary work when it comes to interfacing with the Arduino system.

There are going to be some situations where you would like to take this controller and connect it up to your computer in order to get some more of the work that you would like to do.

Computer interfacing with Arduino is going to be common, but there are still going to be a few steps that we are able to follow to ensure that all of this happens.

The idea of computer interfacing with your Arduino is going to be the best method to choose or work with when you would like to interface the board with your computer.

But it also is going to depend on what cables you would like to use or what is available to you at the time.

While we are here, we need to remember that each of the controllers of Arduino that we work with is able to have a simple connection to the computer if we take the time to use a USB port.

Connecting the Arduino over to the chosen computer is often going to depend on the programming language that we hope to work with, and it will also depend on the add-ons that need to be put onto this controller.

All of that and more can really change up how smoothly the Arduino controller is going to match up with your computer.

As we can imagine already, this is going to be a process that is kind of complicated to work with, and not always easy for a beginner to go through and learn about.

That is why we are going to take some time in this chapter to look at computer interfacing and what all that entails so that we have a better chance of making it work with our own Arduino controllers as well.

The FTDI Chips

One of the things that we need to look at when it comes to computer interfacing is the idea of the FTDI chips.

All of the Arduino boards that you can work with are going to be able to send and receive data, making this data go back and forth from the computer with the help of a USB port, with two main exceptions.

These exceptions are going to be the Mini boards and the Lilypad options.

However, even with those exceptions, you will be able to connect these boards to the computer and get it to interface the way that you want with the help of the FTDI interface.

This is basically going to be a small chip that we can use to help make it easier to exchange data between the computer and the Arduino controller in any manner that you would like.

In other exercises that you can do, it is sometimes possible to work with the Arduino controller in order to go through and read some of the values of the sensors, like the temperature and the light, and then you can see these through the LEDs that are on the board.

But in this chapter, we need to take some time to work with another option, which is going to be known as serial interfacing, which will help us take those values from the sensors and then send them to the computer to make it easier to calculate out all of the information that we need.

That is why we are going to take a look at an example of how we are able to work with the temperature sensors with the help of the serial interface.

We need to make sure that we have a few supplies handy ahead of time, including the Arduino UNO board, a breadboard, and a temperature sensor along with a USB cable.

The code that we are going to need to make all of this happen.

The coding that we can use here will include:

```
const int sensorPin = A0;

int reading;

float voltage;

float temperature;

void setup()
```

```
( Serial.begin(9600);}

Void loop ()

}

Reading = analogRead(sensorPin);

Voltage = reading * 5.0/1024;

Serial.print )voltage);

Serial.printIn("volts");

temperatureC = (voltage – 0.5) * 100;

Serial.printIn("Temperature is");

Serial.print(temperatureC);

Serian.printIn("degrees C")'

Delay(1000);

}
```

After we have been able to verify and then upload the code that we want to work with, we can click on the Serial Monitor that comes up.

You should see that there is a menu that is going to show us the sensor readings of the temperature.

Now we want to use any heat source that we can find in order to raise up the temperature of the device.

Keep in mind that with this device, we are able to handle up to 150 Celsius.

You may also see the (-) symbol show up.

This does not mean that we are working with negative numbers on this one, but it is simply a programming error that is temporary.

While we are going through this, we are able to take a look at more of the parts to see how we are able to get this to come together for our needs and to help us write out our codes.

To start here, we need to look at our Serial.begin(9600) part.

This is going to be the statement that we can write out in order to make sure that we set up all of the necessary communication between the Arduino controller and the computer, using our USB port and cable.

This makes it easier for the two parts to send and receive data from one another.

In addition to this, it is possible to work with two important variables that will need to show up in our code, and these will include the TemperatureC and the voltage, and both of these have to be defined with a float rather than an integer.

This is because the sensor that goes with the temperature is going to be accurate, and then the result has to be a floating number so we can get the complete accuracy, rather than an integer that only works with whole numbers and would require us to do some rounding.

From this point, we need to move on to the next part of our code, which is going to be the part for reading = analogRead(sensorPin);.

This is the instruction that we need to use to help us record the analog input into the right pin of the process.

As we mentioned a bit before, our controller is going to be able to convert the analog signal into a digital value from zero to 1024, and then we are able to use the instruction of voltage = reading * 5/1024.

Now that we are done with this part, we need to go through and do some conversions.

This will allow us to take the values that are digital and change them to a voltage.

The command that we are able to use for this one is going to be Serial.pinrt(voltage).

This is a great option to use because it will send our value effectively over to the computer and can help us to show it up on the IDE of the Arduino when we are ready.

The command that we wrote above is going to be all of the instructions that are system needs so that it can provide us with a value that has "voltage' right behind it to keep things in order.

Then we need to work with the next part of the code, which is going to be the TemperatureC = (voltage − 0.5)*100.

This is important to add to this part because it is going to provide our board with the instructions that it needs in order to take some of the values of voltage to the degree in temperatures.

Remember that we are working with the Celsius scale here and then we are able to go and print out the value to show us what it is.

And then, we finally end up in the last part of the code.

This is going to be the delay(1000).

This is going to be important because it helps us to tell the controller we want it to wait one second before it sends out the temperature and the voltage value to the computer, and then we are able to see the right results of the process.

As we can see, interfacing with the computer is not that difficult of a process to work on.

We just have to be ready to work with it and see all of the neat things that it is able to provide to us along the way.

In the example that we talked about above, with the proper coding, we were able to set up our controller so that it could tell us the temperature based on the voltage, and show that information on our computer, just by combining the controller and the computer together with a USB cable.

That is the beauty of what we are going to see here when we work with this Arduino board, it is not meant to be a difficult process to work with, and after handling a few of the projects of your choice, you will find that it can actually be pretty easy to work with.

Interfacing between the controller and the computer can be simple, and the more projects you do with it, the easier the whole process is going to become.

Chapter 10: The API Functions

When it is time to work with the Arduino board, you will need to take a look at some o the API functions, and all of the great details and features that come with these.

The API that comes with this controller is going to be really rich in features, and all of the different options that a programmer can enjoy will make it just that much easier to work with the device already.

The team that is behind the Arduino computer has done a great job with the API and made sure that it is completely full-featured, providing the programmer with many different options on what they are able to do while tinkering with this controller for their projects.

We are going to spend some time in this chapter taking a look at how we can work with these in more depth so that we can learn about the functions and the features, and see how great this can be for our projects.

The Digital Input and the Output

The first thing on the list to work with is the digital input and output.

There are going to be a number of functions that we can define with the help of the Arduino API, which is going to make it easier to actually communicate and work with the digital pins that are present.

We need to look at the three most common types of these so that we can actually get our board to work.

To help us start with this, though, we need to work with the following code:

pinMode(pin, INPUT – OUTPUT – or INPUT_PULLUP)

This is going to be useful because it allows us to specify a given pin and then designate whether that pin is going to act as an input or if it is going to be output instead.

Newer models of this Arduino are going to be able to have heir pins enabled through the pullup resistors, which is why we added this mode to it as well.

From here, we are able to look at the input and the output for Analog.

In addition to using the digital pins for a lot of our projects, we can also bring in some of the analog pins as well.

These analog pins are going to be useful because they will help us to read through the voltage that other pins are going to provide us.

The readings should be somewhere between 0 and 5 volts.

The upper range is going to be closer to 1023 here, and then we will notice that the lower range will get closer to 0.

The code that we need to use to make sure we are reading through the right pins is analogRead(pin).

This is going to help us to read through the voltage in any pin that we choose to look with.

And then we will get an integer that is between 0 and 1023 like we talked about before.

Or we are able to work with a different code, the analogReference(type), which will then help us to configure this over to voltages instead of giving us the reference point that we need.

The way that we choose to look at these numbers sometimes depends on the board that we are using.

Then it is time for us to move on to a few of the more advanced options that come with the output and input of our Arduino board.

These are not going to fall very close to either of the categories that we have talked about because they will not be analog or digital.

But they will be more advanced categories here, and we can do so much more with the boards when we bring them in.

To start, we have a tone(pint, frequency, OPTIONAL duration).

This one is going to make it so that we are able to specify the given frequency, and then we can generate out a square wave of that frequency onto the pin that we are using.

Then we can work with noTone(pin) that will help us stop the tone that is being generated out of the tone function when we would like.

It is also possible to add a type of pulse to the mix as well.

We could use the code of pulseIn(pin, value) that is going to allow us to read the pulse of any given pin that is there.

If the pin is fluctuating between high and low at this time, then it is going to return the time in microseconds between the high and the low.

Because the pulses may not be completely even at this time, you can actually go through and specify whether you want it to read out the HIGH pulse, or the LOW pulse based on what works the best for what you are doing.

Working With Time

We need to take a little detour here and look at some of the basics of working with time.

This is a function that does work with our board, and they will help us work on any project that is considered time-sensitive, such as making that the scope of our controller.

The first code that we can bring in with this one is known as the delay(value).

We have seen this a few times so far, but the point of using it is that it allows us to pause the sketch we are working on for a certain amount of time.

We can add in the integer value of how long we want the sketch to pause, but keep in mind that this will be done based on milliseconds.

Then we are able to work with a second code that is going to be delayMicrosecond(value).

This is a good code to work with though it has a lot of the same functionality that we saw with the delay() function that we did before.

This one will work in microseconds rather than the milliseconds, so if you need a different time frame to work on here, this is the one to choose.

Working With Math

When it comes to programming, there is going to be a good deal of math.

The math functions that we see with the Arduino API are going to be similar to the math library that comes with the C language, but they are often seen as easier to work with.

This is because you are able to utilize these without needing to actually import the math libraries that you need.

Even if you work on programs that don't need a lot of math in the first place, you can still benefit from these because you never know when it will sneak in.

For the most part, the math that you will work with is simple and will include a lot of the different assignment operators that we talked about earlier.

This can include options like addition, subtraction, multiplication, and division to name a few that you may use.

What Are the Characters?

The next topic that we need to look at is the characters.

While these are rare for this kind of language, it is still important for us to know them any time that we work with a function that is primed for us.

Some of the most common characters that we are able to work with will include:

1. isAlpha(character):

    This one is going to return whether or not the character we are using is alphabetical.

2. islphaNumeric:

    This one is going to give us a character returned even if the character is numeric or alphabetic.

3. isAscii():

    This one is going to let us know whether or not the character is an ASCII character.

4. isControl:

This one is going to let us know whether or not the character is considered a control character.

5. isDigit():

   This is going to return whether or not a character is a number.

6. isGraph():

   This is going to return whether or not the character is something that has visual data.

   Space, for example, is not going to have any of this visual data.

7. isHexidecimalDigit():

   This one is going to let us know whether we are working with hexadecimal or not.

8. isLowerCase():

   This one is going to let us know whether the character is lowercase or not.

9. isPrintable():

   This is going to let us know whether or not the character is one that we are able to print off on a console.

10. isPunct():

This one is going to let us know whether or not the character that we are getting back is a punctuation mark.

11. isSpace():

This one is going to let us know whether the character that we are getting back is a space or not.

12. isUpperCase():

This one is going to let us know whether the character that we are getting returned is an upper case letter.

13. isWhiteSpace():

This one is going to let us know whether the returned character that we are working with is going to be a whitespace character, like a line break, space, or a tab.

Handling Our Random Numbers

We can also work with some of the random numbers.

These random numbers are going to be the functions that we can use to help create random numbers in any program that we write.

We must note with this one though that our computer can never really be all that random or spontaneous though.

This is because all of the parts that we see are going to be based on whatever input the computer gets, and it is going to react in the manner that seems the most logical to it.

The first type of random number that we are able to work with here is going to be the function of randomSeed(number).

This one is going to start up with the generator of a random number so that we can work with that.

We first need to make sure that we feed a number all the way through it, and then it will start again at a random point, which the computer program will choose from the sequence of the pseudo-random number generator's numerical sequence.

We can take this a bit further here and work with the function of random(OPTIONAL minimum, maximum).

This is one that is useful because it can bound together with the generation of the random number.

The maximum value is going to end up being the higher number you are going to allow here, and then the lowest is the lowest number you will allow.

If you do not go through and specify out the minimum you want to work with, then the assumption is that it will be at 0.

A Look at the Bitwise Functions

The final thing that we want to take a look at when it comes to the functions of the Arduino API is the bitwise functions.

These are a specific type of function that is going to make it easier to work with the bytes and the bits of all your codes.

These are going to be considered the smallest parts of data that the computer can actually work with.

There are arguments that there are some smaller data types, but for our practical purposes, this is where we need to go with the smallest parts.

Some of the different bitwise functions that we are able to use with Arduino include:

1. bit(bitNum):

   This one is going to provide us with the value of a given bit.

2. bitClear(variable, bit):

   This one is going to be how we set the given bit of a specified numerical variable to 0.

3. bitRead(variable, bit):

This is going to give back the bit of a specified numeric variable.

4. bitSet(variable, bit):

   This is going to set a given variable's bit like the position denoted by bit to 1.

5. bitWrite9(variable, bit, 0 or 1):

   This one will set the bit at the given position inside of the variable to either be at 0 or 1, depending on what you set in the code.

6. highByte(value):

   This one is going 0 return to us the highest byte of a given value that we have.

7. lowByte(value):

   This one is going to be the opposite of before, and it is going to return the lowest byte of the value that you choose to look at.

As we can already see here, there are a ton of different functions that we are able to use when it comes to the API that is part of Arduino.

Learning what all of these can do for us and exploring them in more detail is going to make a huge difference in what we are able to do with these as well.

As you get more familiar with the Arduino controller and all of the neat things that it is able to do, you will quickly see why this is a great option to work with, and you will be able to see these functions doing some actual work in the process as well.

Chapter 11: The Stream Class and Arduino

Now it is time for us to move on to a new topic that we can explore in more detail as well.

In this chapter, we are going to work with the stream class, which is a bit different than what we have done before.

But if you are looking to work with strings in our coding, then we need to get a better idea of how the stream class is going to work for our needs.

You will find that the stream class is a fairly simple concept to work with, especially once we go through it a little bit more.

Despite its simplicity, though, we need to make sure that we realize how important it is to work with.

The stream class, when we work on it by itself, is going to be based on working through reading information from our chosen source, and then having this be the way that you design the sketch that you want to work with.

Since the stream is going to be all about reading the data, it is also important that we talk about using the keyboard and the mouse on this kind of class, even though these may not be related directly to the topic.

Hook up the keyboard and the mouse now because they will make the whole process a bit easier.

When you decide to work with this data, especially when you are getting all of the data prepared and ready to go, you will find that there are times when the character sets we want to work with are going to be a bit longer, such as enough characters to make a whole sentence.

The whole idea that comes with the string is that it will help us to handle this work on aboard.

Strings are going just to be sets of character values that are linked together in a manner that is similar to an array.

This means that they will be considered contiguous in the memory of our board, and when the computer takes a look at how this works, they will see them as one long and interconnected unit.

Working with the strings will simply mean that we need to take the time to learn how we can manipulate these units, as well as the abilities of the board, which will allow us to do this.

When we just look at the simplicity of the string, it is easy enough to understand.

Strings are just going to be what we know as character arrays.

This means that we are still going to find these strings to look like they are a part of the C language here, so if you have some experience with this language, you should notice how easy this is supposed to work.

Keep in mind that the strings here because of this are going to have some low-level abstraction that we need to work with.

For example, in many of the more modern languages or programming, the strings are not really going to be revealed in the character as one of these arrays.

Instead of working with these, they are going to be seen as an abstract object instead.

Even if they are seen as a character array in this, they will still be treated in this way.

A string is going to be easy to work with and is just composed of the n + 1 characters, where our n is going to be how many letters are found in that string in general.

So, if you are looking to make a string out o the word "hello" then we would know that we are working with six characters.

The reason that we have six characters instead of five is that the end is going to be a null terminating character, which will help the compiler know that the end of the array has been reached and that we are all done with this part of the code.

In addition to some of the work that we talked about above, it is possible to go through and define the string in a manner that is similar to how we are used to defining the array.

You can use this to make them bigger than the string that you plan to put into them as well.

When you go through this process of defining an array, you have to provide it with a value right off the bat, but it is also possible to start it off simple and just give it the size that you think should be there and then expand that out later on if it is not right or your needs.

This is one of the ways to make our strings more dynamic, while still allowing us to make some changes to what will happen to them later when we want to go through and do some of the rewritings that are necessary later on.

Now, as a programmer who is just getting started, all of this information is going to be important due to the fact that strings are fundamental and important to a lot of the different programs that you would like to use when handling information in your code.

This is especially true for those who would like to be able to handle the input and any of the output of a specific file that you are working on at the time.

Through this guidebook, we have been able to take some time to look through all of this and how it is going to work.

But now we need to take this a bit further and learn how we are able to go through this and define our strings.

The best coding that we can use to make this a reality is the following:

```
char myString[6] = "hello";
```

You can then spend some time referring to this entire string at a later point with the name of the character.

Most of the data that is worked with by the board is going to be worked with in terms of how many bytes it is, and most of the actual textual data is going to be worked with in terms of C strings because it is easy to parse these characters when you would like.

One final thing to note here is that we are going to need some time to learn more about these parts and how they work.

And over time, we are going to be able to learn the exact right way to use these and to treat the strings so that they will do more of what we want along the way.

There are a lot of times when we need to work with the strings in our codes, and knowing how to use these, and how we can make these work for our own needs is going to be really important.

Take some time to look at how these strings work, along with some of the characters that come with them, to ensure that we are able to use them in the right manner as well.

Chapter 12: Creating Our Own User-Defined Functions

The final thing that we need to take a look at when it comes to coding in the Arduino board is how to work with some of our own user-defined functions.

In any coding language, there are going to be some functions that are built-in.

We are able to pull these out at any time that we would like to use them, and they are there for the taking to do with as we want.

But then there are also times when we want to create our own functions, special functions that are able to handle a ton of the work that we need but are special to the specific codes that we are trying to write out for our program.

And these second types of functions are going to be known as user-defined functions.

Functions are going to be important in many of the codes that we want to write in this language and in other languages as well.

They are good at making sure that our code is organized and clean and that we are actually able to reuse some parts of the code if we would like.

It is even there to help us to make sure that the code is going to behave in the manner that we want along the way.

Basically, these functions are going to be just simple tools that we are able to use, and that are created to help serve the particular actions that we want inside of our codes, just like we would guess from the name.

While we have actually looked at a few codes through this guidebook that is going to have functions inside of them already, it is time for us to actually look into some of the details that come with these, ensuring that we will have a better understanding of how these work and why we would want to use them as well.

This is going to make it easier or us to explain some of the features that we may have missed out on and didn't understand when we first got started because we were not talking about the functions in the first place back then.

So, let's dive into the functions and what we are able to do with this.

The first step here is to take a closer look at how we can declare any of the functions that are on our list to work with.

This is an important step when we work with our own user-defined functions, so we need to make sure that we are doing it in the proper manner on our programs.

A good example of some of the code that we can use for this includes:

float employeeEarnings (float hoursWorked, float payrate) {

float results: // this will be the value that we are going to return when this function has been called up. We want to make sure that it is going to match the type of data that we are using before the name of the function

results = hoursWorked * payrate

Return results // return tells the function that it needs to send a value back once to where it was originally called.

}

As you take a look over this, open up the compiler that you are using with Arduino and try typing it in.

You should also look at the code and see what it is actually able to offer in terms of what we can do with it, and even what you can already understand from that code based on some of the other topics that we have discussed in this guidebook.

You may be surprised at how many of the other parts you are going to recognize based on what we have had some time to talk about in this guidebook, and what we have been able to do so far.

This function above is going to be a good one to work with because it is able to take on two arguments, and has to be able to do this in order to complete its tasks successfully.

This is going to have two arguments, including the hoursWorked and the payrate that it has to handle in order to get things taken care of.

It also is able to take some time to work on a bit of the simple math that we brought up earlier, before bringing up some kind of floating number as the value, based on the numbers that are there.

The return that we will be able to get with this one is going to help us to either end or we can terminate our function and then send back the value that was placed with us, which should happen right after we use the word of return, which is going to be a variable as the results of the calculations that we worked on before.

All of this is going to be completed in order to help us better understand how these functions are supposed to work and how we can actually go through and do some work with them.

This may seem like a lot of information, but when we have all of this in mind, it is then time for us to go through and call up all of the functions.

This is going to make it easier for us to see what the earnings of the employers are, and it can often make things easier so that we can see what will happen in this process as we move along with it all and actually bring in some of the user-defined functions.

To help us make a bit more sense out of this and what we are trying to do, we need to use the following code to help:

void loop () {

floathoursWorked = 37.5;

float payRate = 18.50;

float result = employeeEarnings (hoursWorked, payRate)

// results will be 693.75

This is a pretty straightforward cod that we are able to work with, but it is definitely going to show us what we are able to do here, and why all of the parts are going to be important along the way.

It is also a simple way to get some ideas on how the function is going to work overall.

Now, when we get here the first thing that we are going to find in all of this is the function that we need to declare, and we need to make sure that this is declared independent of and outside of all the other functions.

This means that we need to be able to take some time to write out the code for any function that we would like to create, and it needs to be done either inside of the setup function or the loop function that we are working with.

You can then take some time to work on other functions that are defined by the user from that point.

It is also possible for us to take a look at a second example of what we can do to make this so much easier to work with functions that are defined by the user.

We will find that the following sketch is going to be useful here and will help us out with a lot of the times when we need to write out these kinds of functions while making sure that the readings we get out of the sensors are as smooth as possible.

The sketch that we can use to make this one happen includes:

```
int sensorSmoothin (analogPin) {

in sensorValue = 0;

for (int index = 0; index < 5, index ++)

digitalWrite(LED_BUILTIN, HIGH); //Turn on the LED for smoothing.

sensorValue= sensorValue + analogRead (analogPin)

delay(100) // 100 millisecond delay between the samples

}

digitalWrite(LED_BUILTIN, LOW); //turn off the LED
```

sensorValue = sensorValue / 5 //average the values over five samples that we are using.

return sensorValue;

}

As you go through some of this, you are going to find that this is going to show up a lot of the functions that we were talking about earlier on.

This is going to make it so much easier for us to feel comfortable with some of the work that we are trying to do along the way.

The more time that you spend working on some of the codings that we want to do along the way, the easier it is to work with the code because we are comfortable and can recognize things along the way.

Keep in mind that this is going to be a really good function to work with simply because it is the one that will smooth out all of the input that we receive from the data heading our way from all of the sensors.

This is going to be especially true if you find that there are some inclinations that the inputs will be a bit jittery and not all that organized as we go through the process.

The reason that this is going to be a process that works well is that it is able to come in and average out the sample a bit, giving us a more consistent data flow in the process.

We are able to take a closer look at the code that we wrote out above and will see that it is pretty similar to what we did at the beginning of this chapter, with a few key changes that make it work better here.

Let's dive in for a moment to see what all got changed and why that matters.

With this particular code, we are going to start out by initializing the sensorValue variable that is found in the code.

The reason that we do this is so that this variable is able to call up the function of sensorSmoothing() that we need for this part.

This is going to happen on analog pin 0, thanks to how our code is set up and can help us because we will end up with the average of the results, rather than focusing on just one result at a time along the way.

So, instead of having us just focus on the one, we had it average the input over the five samples that were in use.

Of course, there are a few cautions that we need to pay attention to here, and we have to remember that the functions we are trying to work with here are not going to always be smooth, and there are times when the functions are a bit more complicated to work with.

The functions may not even need to come with a return variable or parameters to work either, and this adds on another layer to the complexity that we are working with here. All that this is going to do is that when you bring them up, they will execute the lines of code that you want.

Then you have the freedom to go through and terminate it all before bringing the compiler back to the place in the code where you tried to call them from in the first place.

And that is all there is to the process.

As we can see already, these functions that are defined by the user here are not really that complicated to work with, and they open the doors to a lot of other coding options that you are able to do on a regular basis if you would like.

Whether you decide to work with some of the functions that are automatically found in the language library you are using, or you decide to define some of your own, you will find that these functions are going to have a really important part in the process as you go along writing codes.

And the goal of working with them in this chapter is to make sure that you know exactly how you can go through and work with some of the functions on your own, and create some of your own, no matter what kinds of codes and programs you are trying to create in the first place.

Conclusion

Thank you for making it through to the end of **Arduino Programming for Beginners**, let's hope it was informative and able to provide you with all of the tools you need to achieve your goals whatever they may be.

The next step is to purchase your first Arduino controller and get to work with some of your own programming needs as well.

There are a ton of different things that we are able to do when it comes to working with the Arduino controller, and this guidebook will take some time to dive into it, and help us explore how, even as a beginner, we are able to get this to work out great for our needs.

Inside this guidebook, we went over all of the different parts that we need to know in order to get started with using the Arduino board for our own needs.

We took a look at what this board is all about, some of the benefits of working with this board, and so much more.

It is such a great option to work with overall, and if you want to learn how to do programming and more without needing a lot of hefty and expensive equipment, then this is the option to spend your time on.

With this in mind, we also dived a bit more into some of the specifics of what we are able to do with this board.

We looked at the Arduino language and what we are able to do with it some of the operators and the logical statements, how to get the board to make some of the statements that it wants on its own, and even how the C language is able to fit into here and make a difference as well.

There are a lot of people who want to get into the world of programming and learn how to make this work for tier own needs as well.

They find that having the ability to work with a programming tool that is easy to handle and can do all of the work that they want is one of the best options for their needs.

And the Arduino board is one of the best tools that we can use to make sure this happens.

This guidebook took the time to explore this controller and all of the neat things that even beginners can use it for, without all of the costs.

When you are ready to get on board with learning to do some basic programming and even design some of your own cool pieces of technology, then the Arduino system is the right one for your needs.

Make sure to check out this guidebook to learn the steps and the programming that you need in order to turn this into a reality and ensure that you are able to get the best results overall.

Finally, if you found this book useful in any way, a review on Amazon is always appreciated!

CPSIA information can be obtained
at www.ICGtesting.com
Printed in the USA
LVHW051433201120
672130LV00008B/482